Playing for Rangers No 13

PLAYING FOR RANGERS NO 13

Edited by Ken Gallacher

Stanley Paul
London Melbourne Sydney Auckland Johannesburg

Stanley Paul & Co. Ltd

An imprint of the Hutchinson Publishing Group

17-21 Conway Street, London W1P 5HL

Hutchinson Group (Australia) Pty Ltd
30-32 Cremorne Street, Richmond South, Victoria 3121
PO Box 151, Broadway, New South Wales 2007

Hutchinson Group (NZ) Ltd
32-34 View Road, PO Box 40-086, Glenfield, Auckland 10

Hutchinson Group (SA) (Pty) Ltd
PO Box 337, Bergvlei 2012, South Africa

First published 1981
© Stanley Paul & Co. Ltd 1981

Set in Baskerville

Printed in Great Britain by the Anchor Press Ltd
and bound by Wm Brendon & Son Ltd
both of Tiptree, Essex

British Library Cataloguing in Publication Data

Playing for Rangers. – No. 13
  1. Rangers Football Club – Periodicals
  796.334′63′0941443   GV943.6.G/

ISBN 0 09 146071 9

Black and white photographs by Sportapics
Colour photographs: Rangers with the Cup, the Cup Final
goal, Ally Dawson, Colin Jackson and Davie Cooper by
Sportapics; others by Colorsport

Frontispiece:
Goalkeeper Jim Stewart jumps to clutch this high cross ball from the
head of Morton forward Jim Tolmie

CONTENTS

DREAMS OF GLORY

It went to a replay, the Scottish Cup Final last season, when the experts made Rangers the underdogs as they faced the exciting talents of Dundee United.

Yet, at the end of it all, Rangers triumphed by 4–1 and these goals and the manner of their victory brought celebrations to the legions of fans across the world. More important it carried Rangers forward into Europe and into the tournament where they have known most success – the European Cup Winners' Cup.

It is in this competition that Rangers have twice been beaten finalists, against Fiorentina of Italy in a two-legged final in those far off days of 1961, the first year of the tournament; then again when they lost after extra time to the Bayern Munich team of Franz Beckenbauer and Gerd Muller when the final was played in Nuremberg in 1967. And it is in this competition that Rangers finally won a European trophy when they went to Barcelona to beat Moscow Dynamo in 1972.

They had qualified for Europe before beating Dundee United. They would have taken a place in the UEFA Cup if they had lost the final. But Rangers wanted a trophy to show for their season and they wanted a place in the more prestigious of the two competitions. They won both. . . .

And after doing so they looked ahead to that tournament which they have graced so often in the past.

This is the stuff dreams are made of. The Rangers team, so many of them without experience of European games, can dream now of following in the footsteps of the men who have gone before and others who remain alongside them to pass on their so valuable experience.

The tradition of Rangers demands that they be involved in

Last season's dreams of glory began to take shape here at Broomfield with this opening Scottish Cup goal from Gregor Stevens (*left*). He turns away to receive congratulations from his team-mates after his header beat Airdrie keeper John Martin

winning – and involved in Europe. Their proud history is littered with trophies and with the scalps of famous teams from the Continent who have come to Ibrox to strut across that famous turf and then learned to their cost that the Rangers cannot be taken lightly. There is an atmosphere about European football which is not captured elsewhere – not in the tension of an Old Firm game, nor in the most dramatic of League matches, nor even in the drama of a Cup Final. Last year Rangers missed out on Europe. This year they qualified again and the memories of recent years rolled back to thrill the fans and quicken the pulses of those who will want to see the European greats parade their skills at Ibrox again.

In John Greig's first year at Ibrox there were famous victories over the Italian champions Juventus, the Dutch champions PSV Eindhoven and then a quarter final defeat from the crack West German team, Cologne. The following season Valencia with Mario Kempes and Rainer Bonhof came to Glasgow and

Frank Kopel chases the ball as goalkeeper Hamish McAlpine watches anxiously. But the chase is in vain and Davie Cooper, on the right, puts Rangers on the road to victory with the first goal in the Final replay

Rangers lost – but who would ever forget the magical way that Kempes, that brilliant Argentinian, brought about the defeat?

That is what Europe means – memories, either of glory or of defeat, but usually unforgettable.

And Europe has a habit of bringing players together. For a few days they live together, eat together, work together without a break and all of that builds team morale more than the weekly grind of League football at home can do.

It was significant last season that when John Greig decided on a mid-season break for his players they responded by coming home and improving their performances. It was no accident. The break had worked. At that time results had been poor, criticism had been severe, the League title was rushing out of their grasp. Greig, knowing how much the team had missed these European games, suddenly decided that a Continental tonic was needed. Off the team went to Portugal. They didn't play a glamour game. It was not against Benfica or even old rivals Sporting Club but against the local Estoril team who topped the Portuguese Second Division. But Rangers did win and they did try out fresh ideas which they had not been able to use at home in the intensely competitive Premier League. These ideas were put to use on their return and after they came

One of the players who knew the days of European glory, Willie Johnston helped Rangers win the European Cup Winners' Cup in 1972. Last season's comeback man takes the ball past Airdrie's Harry Cairney

home they lost just twice – to St Mirren at Love Street by an odd goal and to Celtic at Ibrox by the only goal of the game. But for the rest they showed enormous improvement, the rot in results in the League was halted sufficiently to allow them to finish third. And the Scottish Cup which had become their main target was won. Those four days in Portugal proved to be four very vital days for Greig and his players and they were not slow to emphasize that as the season reached its thrilling Hampden climax.

But dreams do not end with Scottish Cup wins, nor with thoughts of European glory. Dreams at Ibrox are never ending because every season throws up its own challenges and every season Rangers are expected not only to meet these challenges but to overcome them.

John Greig, captain for so many years, has always known that. Now he occupies the manager's chair he is not allowed to forget it. Not that he would want to. After twenty-one years devoted to Ibrox Greig wants more and more glory for the club which has been his life.

In his three years as manager the club has won the Scottish Cup twice, the League Cup, been runners up in the Scottish Cup once and in the League Championship once. But Greig won't rest until he wins the title. And when he does that he won't rest until he has won another title. That is the way with Rangers. . .it has always been and always will be a constant search for glory.

Last season brought a taste. . .this season must bring another taste. . .and every season after that cannot be without the dreams of glory which have made Rangers the legendary club they are.

The man who made all the dreams come true on that unforgettable Hampden night – wing star Davie Cooper. Here he is beating a despairing tackle from Dundee United's Eamonn Bannon

'We're on our way to Hampden' the fans were singing at Broomfield when Rangers beat Airdrie 5–0 in the first round proper of the Scottish Cup. This was goal number four, from Derek Johnstone the lone Ranger in the picture, which Airdrie full back Harry Cairney failed to stop

GLORY IN THE SCOTTISH CUP

When the draw for the first round proper of the Scottish Cup was made on 3 January not many Rangers' fans would have predicted with any hope that it would be their team's year in the tournament.

For the second time that season at the grim, tight, little ground of Broomfield, Rangers had been held to a draw by the part-timers of Airdrie. It had happened in the first Premier League match of the year . . . now it had happened again, just before the draw paired the teams in the Cup. The battles at Broomfield had been hard, dour struggles and now Rangers had to return there with the Cup a glittering far-off prize away in the distance.

But that first match in the Cup was to be just one of the troublesome hurdles that Rangers had to clear before that marvellous Scottish Cup Final replay brought them the trophy.

It was a long campaign, marked by some of Rangers' best football of the season, and also by stumbles which brought them close to disaster!

Yet, back to that first Cup match, and the pressures which built up for the Rangers players as they moved towards their confrontation with former Ibrox player Bobby Watson's side.

The shrewd Watson talked of the game with confidence. Why not? He had little to lose. His players, training a couple of nights a week, had done so much better than he had ever hoped in their first season in the Top Ten. Even that early they seemed safe from relegation – and they did stay up – so the part-timers who made up the Airdrie side looked on the Cup as a bonus.

For Rangers it was so different. By that time, just after the turn of the year, their chances of the League title had started to disappear. They had lost out in the League Cup. The one prize which seemed open to them was the Scottish Cup and it was unthinkable that Ibrox could go a second season in succession without a major honour to adorn the trophy room.

Watson's pre-match talk was designed to add to the pressure on Rangers and when 18,000 people crammed their way into

13

More action from that glory day at Broomfield as Derek Johnstone tries to power his way past Airdrie's Jim March

the ground the Rangers fans, who made up the bulk of the crowd, were there hoping that their heroes could at least earn a draw and then win the replay at Ibrox.

What a welcome surprise waited for them! Rangers went on to take control of the game from the beginning. The stuffy Airdrie team were not given time to settle into their normally defensive set up. Instead Rangers took the initiative and with one of their more memorable performances hammered in five goals. Gregor Stevens, Ian Redford, Jim Bett and Derek Johnstone with two were the men who grabbed the goals.

It had, however, been a team performance, one which delighted manager John Greig and also planted the seeds of hope in the minds of the fans that this was to be Rangers' year in the Cup.

But the next round brought them closer to disaster than any other game they played during the season. Again the draw took them away from Ibrox. This time they had to go to Muirton Park at Perth where a tidy St Johnstone team, under the management of another ex-Ranger Alex Rennie, were battling for

Ian Redford in full flight – it was his goal which saved Rangers at Muirton against St Johnstone

promotion at the top of the First Division. On paper it looked a tough one, just as tough as Airdrie was reckoned to be before the match.

Yet when Colin McAdam and Ian Redford put Rangers two goals up the stage seemed set for another romp towards Hampden and that distant Final. Then dramatically everything changed. Jim Docherty scored one for St Johnstone and then as goalkeeper Peter McCloy struggled John Brogan added another two! Incredibly Rangers were a goal down with just eight minutes left to save the game. When Colin McAdam scored with two minutes to go only to see the goal disallowed, Rangers' fans began to trudge sadly from the Muirton terracings. Then came the 'saver' . . . a cross from Davie Cooper, a header from Ian Redford and in the dying seconds Rangers snatched another chance in the Cup.

That goal was to be worth hundreds of thousands of pounds to Rangers. It kept the team in the tournament which eventually carried them into Europe.

There was still the replay to come but John Greig admitted

afterwards: 'I thought it was all over when the goal was disallowed. There was no way of coming back from that . . . or so it seemed. That goal alone repays Ian Redford's transfer fee.'

Four days later St Johnstone travelled to Ibrox but the fight had gone from them and while teenage wonder boy Ally McCoist scored they didn't look like bringing off any more shocks. Rangers coasted to victory with goals from Colin McAdam, an Alex Caldwell own goal, and a third from Gregor Stevens.

The reward was a home tie against Hibs, the team at the top of the First Division, and the huge Rangers support cast envious eyes across the city to Parkhead where Celtic had now been drawn against three of the bottom teams in the First Division.

One time Celtic star Bertie Auld had left Partick Thistle to manage Hibs and they had been rejuvenated since his take over. The threat posed by them was one that the Rangers players were only too well aware of. Possibly because of Auld's presence

Despite a season during which he was ordered off three times Gregor Stevens, seen here tackling Morton's Jim Tolmie, was superb in the Scottish Cup – and the rugged defender scored two goals en route to Hampden!

Jim Bett (*right*) picks himself up after Dundee United goalkeeper
Hamish McAlpine saved his extra time shot in the Scottish Cup
Final. Other United players are defender Frank Kopel and
Davie Dodds (11)

and also because Hibs, despite being in the First Division, still
remain a glamour team, 27,000 people were at Ibrox to see the
quarter final tie.

Again Rangers kept one of their most professional performances for the Cup. Rarely under pressure they won 3–1, their
goals coming from Robert Russell, Colin McAdam and John
MacDonald while veteran Jacky McNamara got the Hibs consolation goal.

Now fate was good to Rangers. For as they went into the
semi-final draw with Celtic, Dundee United and either Morton
or Clydebank, the Ibrox team were landed with the easier task.
Celtic, the holders, were drawn against League Cup winners
Dundee United at Hampden while Rangers were to meet the
winners of the Morton-Clydebank match, at Parkhead.

That quarter final went to a second replay before Premier
League side Morton qualified for the last four. It was in the

build up to the semi-final that Greig's thoroughness in preparation paid off. Both replays were watched and then every other game Morton played before the clash at Parkhead came under the scrutiny of either the Ibrox boss or one of his coaching staff. Nothing was to be left to chance with Hampden and the Cup now so close.

In the event, Rangers scarcely allowed Morton a try at goal. The Cappielow side did score but that was with a late Andy Ritchie penalty and by then Rangers were ahead with goals from Colin Jackson and Robert Russell.

But it was a bad semi-final, scarred by fifty fouls and Morton having two players sent off and five booked by referee Brian McGinlay. Rangers had three players booked in the mayhem that afternoon but the most important thing of all for the Ibrox fans in the 28,000 crowd was that the team was back at Hampden for the sixth Scottish Cup Final in succession!

Meanwhile they still didn't know their opponents, for Celtic and Dundee United drew at Hampden. Then, four days later in the replay while Rangers were beating St Mirren in a Premier League game at Ibrox, Dundee United beat Celtic 3–2 and Rangers realized that they were facing the great provincial hopes in the Hampden Final on 9 May.

Dundee United had already won the League Cup – for the second year in a row! Now they had beaten Celtic in the semi-final of the Scottish Cup and doubts about their ability to rise to the challenge of the big occasion were being swept away. Ibrox boss John Greig had frequently voiced his admiration for United and for their manager Jim McLean, brother of Rangers veteran Tommy.

As the build up to the Final began McLean debunked the myths which surrounded his side's form in Glasgow – and against Rangers, in particular. He stressed: 'We beat Rangers 4–1 at Ibrox in a League game so they know exactly what we can do. Then we matched Celtic once and beat them the second time at Hampden. That's added to our win at Parkhead in the League Cup semi-final! So why should we worry about playing in Glasgow any more?

'I think Rangers can worry about us after that win we had at Ibrox.'

Ian Redford just before striking that last minute penalty, with Hamish McAlpine ready to lunge to his right

The ball has struck McAlpine's legs and bounced high in the air as an open-mouthed Redford watches in torment

It's too easy, Hamish McAlpine appears to be saying, as he fields this ball with a grounded Ian Redford and Jim Bett the only two Rangers in sight

Naturally, Rangers did worry. But in the Ibrox dressing-room they had their own secret weapon, a man who knew Jim McLean's mind as well as anyone. Little Tommy McLean read the quotes from his big brother Jim and allowed himself some quiet chuckles.

He knew that, despite what Jim said publicly about the game, he did worry over his team's performances in Glasgow. He knew that Jim was haunted by the fact that his record against Rangers was not a good one.

He knew that Jim would be worried about this game, playing it over and over again in his mind and agonising about the players he would select.

Eventually, however, Jim McLean did decide on his team. Twenty-four hours before the Final he named the men who had beaten Celtic in the semi-final: McAlpine; Holt, Kopel; Phillip, Hegarty, Narey; Bannon, Milne, Kirkwood, Sturrock, Dodds.

It was formidable – but, at Troon, where Rangers stayed for their final preparations, John Greig was glad to hear that it was exactly the team he had predicted. And to keep himself ahead in the battle of wits which would decide the destination of the trophy, Greig kept his line up secret until the teams went out at Hampden the next day. He was criticized for that but maintained defiantly: 'I am trying to win the Cup for Rangers and for the fans and if this gives me an advantage then I'll take that advantage. I don't care about criticism – all I care about is what is best for Rangers!'

When Greig did announce the team Derek Johnstone, their deposed club captain, was left sitting in the stand and Davie Cooper and John MacDonald were on the bench. the team was: Stewart; Jardine, Dawson; Stevens, Forsyth, Bett; McLean, Russell, McAdam, Redford, W. Johnston.

Amazingly the Rangers team contained fewer players with experience of a Hampden final than the United team. It was a first final for goalkeeper Jim Stewart, for midfield men Jim Bett and Ian Redford and for striker Colin McAdam. Not surprisingly nerves and uncertainty showed up. Not surprisingly, either, John Greig elected for caution after all the experts had gone for a Dundee United victory. Sandy Jardine spent most of his time behind his two central defenders, 'sweeping' there in Continental style to foil the bursts of Paul Sturrock and Davie

The tension catches up with Rangers' boss John Greig in the Hampden dug out as he hurls instructions to his players. Coach Joe Mason is on the left

Experience tells! Right back Sandy Jardine edges ahead of Dundee United striker Willie Pettigrew to take the ball cleanly from his toes

Dodds. The strategy worked. United were curbed and while Jim Stewart had one marvellous save from an Eamonn Bannon free kick and another good save from Billy Kirkwood, the Tannadice team rarely threatened.

The trouble was that neither did Rangers . . . though they did have the best chance of all to win the game. Ian Redford the star of that last minute drama at Perth against St Johnstone was pushed into the late, late limelight once more. This time, though, he didn't walk off the field with his arms upraised in salute. Instead he slumped to the ground in anguish after failing to win the trophy for Rangers in a fateful eighty-ninth minute.

Until then Rangers had hardly had a shot at goal – one from Jim Bett into the side net and then two more tries which Dave Narey cleared off the line with Hamish McAlpine beaten. It was soon after that the penalty arrived. There was no doubt about the award when Iain Phillip sent Robert Russell tumbling in the box. Up came Redford who had scored against United at Ibrox with a penalty just weeks before. He hit the ball to Hamish McAlpine's left – the keeper dived to his right but somehow he managed to raise his legs, the ball cannoned from them and was cleared. The whistle blew. The game ended. And Redford held his head while his team-mates consoled him, the Rangers fans chanted his name from the terracings and the rival managers came on to ready the players for extra time. It was the first ever penalty miss by Redford but as manager John Greig said after extra time had left the teams still locked together at 0–0 – 'No one blames Ian. We don't forget that if it hadn't been for his goal in the last minute against St Johnstone at Perth we wouldn't even be at Hampden today.'

So the 53,000 fans left without seeing a goal, knowing that the teams had to return to Hampden three days later; and knowing, too, that managers Greig and McLean promised better things from the replay.

In the end just one of those promises came true – Greig's promise to the red, white and blue hordes who follow, follow Rangers.

Greig was aware that his players had shown the kind of caution that the fans didn't want to see. He hammered that point home to his players on the eve of the replay. 'We cannot go into a Cup Final on the retreat,' he insisted. 'That is not the way that Rangers can approach big games. There will be a different attitude in the replay. I'll make sure of that.'

He did so with his team selection, and the players then carried out the promise on the Hampden pitch. Greig's team that Tuesday night was: Stewart; Jardine, Dawson; Stevens, Forsyth,

It's an earlier game against lesser opposition, Forfar Athletic, but Davie Cooper shows the style which made him a Hampden hit in the Final replay

Bett; Cooper, Russell, D. Johnstone, Redford, MacDonald. The two places on the bench went to Tommy McLean and Colin McAdam. Willie Johnston was injured in the first game and could not be considered for the replay. But while United boss Jim McLean stuck by the same team, Greig had made bold changes. Davie Cooper and John MacDonald had brought dash and verve to Rangers' attacks in the late stages of the first game. Now they went on from the beginning. It was a brave move by Greig and one which clearly caught out that shrewd tactician Jim McLean. He expected Rangers to play the same way, instead he was caught by an attacking hurricane.

Cooper was the man who did the damage. The often moody, but always skilled winger had the best game of his Rangers career. After only ten minutes he had given Rangers the lead. After another ten minutes he was fouled, took the kick himself and floated a ball across for Robert Russell to get the second.

Three minutes later Davie Dodds scored for United – but that was only a pause in the march towards glory by Cooper and Rangers. In the twenty-ninth minute he master-minded the move which brought young John MacDonald the third goal. It was a perfectly placed, perfectly weighted pass which slashed open the United defence and left MacDonald clear to score. It was a goal which will remain in the memories of the 43,099 fans who were there to see it. In the second half MacDonald scored a fourth after a pass from Ian Redford gave him the chance and Rangers had won the Scottish Cup easily.

It was their twenty-fourth victory in the competition and the first time that skipper Ally Dawson had gone up to collect the trophy. But it was Cooper's night and manager Greig said afterwards: 'Davie Cooper showed so much class, so much sheer skill, that it was a delight to watch him. We had to attack United's back four. The way Coop and John MacDonald played when they came on in the first game decided me to give them their chance from the beginning this time. That paid off for us.'

The difference, too, was in attitude. This was a Rangers team

Scottish international star Dave Narey can do nothing as John MacDonald scores for Rangers in the Cup Final replay

playing without fear; a Rangers team pushing forward trying to get the goals that mean so much to the fans. One after-match quote from Greig underlined that when he pointed out: 'Near the end of the game I wasn't wanting them to take any chances. I was looking for young John MacDonald to take the ball to the corner flags when he picked it up. But the boy was looking for his hat trick. He still wanted goals.'

Basically, they had all wanted goals. And glory. Both arrived that Hampden night. If the victory was a boost for Rangers, the performance was a boost for the game in Scotland as a whole. The first game had been dogged by the fear of losing. It had been a tactical battle, interesting perhaps, but not exciting. The second game had all the excitement that the people on the terracings crave. It had thrown up superb individual performances from Davie Cooper and John MacDonald. It had thrown up goals and it had thrown up entertainment.

Above all, for Rangers fans it had brought the Scottish Cup back to Ibrox. That meant that the trophy room would not be empty and that the team would be playing in the glamour laden European Cup Winners' Cup as a double reward for their famous victory.

Robert Russell, another goal scorer in that famous 4–1 victory over Dundee United, demonstrates his skills here as he evades a tackle from Kilmarnock's Ian Gibson

MY IBROX DREAM
by Jim Stewart

I haven't checked the record books, but even without looking at them I'm fairly sure that I set some kind of Scottish Cup record last season.

You see, I won a winner's medal after playing in only two games, the semi-final against Morton and then the Final against Dundee United. And that Final came only a couple of months after I was playing on a works park for the Middlesbrough reserve team!

So you can see why I still pinch myself to make sure that all that has happened to me is true. Even the night that I heard Rangers wanted me I didn't quite believe it. I was at home in Middlesbrough when John Neal, the manager at Ayresome Park then, phoned to say that Rangers manager John Greig had made an offer which he was ready to accept. I'd been dozing in a chair when the phone rang and the next morning I had to ask my wife if I'd been dreaming. It had come so much out of the blue that I couldn't grasp it.

There had been talk before, rumour after rumour that Rangers wanted me, Aberdeen wanted me, other clubs in England wanted me, but nothing had materialized. So there I was a Scottish international goalkeeper, with two caps to my credit, playing away in the Middlesbrough reserve team. I was a bit unlucky, I suppose, being down there at the same time as the Northern Ireland keeper Jim Platt.

To begin with when Boro bought me from Kilmarnock for £100,000 things were fine. Then I made a mistake or two and Jim was brought into the team. I didn't get many chances after that. Once when he was injured I got a game and then, again, when he was with the Irish squad I played on the club's close-season tour of Japan. Then when last season started Jim was back in the League side. I didn't blame the Boss because Jim had been a star in the Irish side which took the British International Championship, and also it was his testimonial year with the club.

I understood all that – but it didn't help my career any! I

did, in fact, ask John Neal for a move and he was understanding about it. That's when I heard rumours about Aberdeen and about one or two English clubs. Then after a season of playing in the North Midlands League against reserve teams from Doncaster, Rotherham, Halifax and Lincoln this bid from Rangers arrived. Just the week before I had been playing against the Lincoln second string on a works pitch and then suddenly I was catapulted into the big time at Ibrox.

Moving from a works pitch to the magnificent Ibrox stadium was unbelievable. I hadn't seen the new look Ibrox until I came home and I was pushed straight into the first team against Dundee United in a Premier League game. It wasn't the best debut – United won 4–1 – but the fans were tremendous to me and they have stayed that way since.

Mind you I was able to forget that defeat eventually when we won the Scottish Cup after a replay against Dundee United – and beat them by the same score!

That Cup medal was really something for me. The furthest I'd ever gone in the Cup during my years with Kilmarnock was the quarter finals. That was the year before I was sold to Middlesbrough and we knocked Celtic out of the tournament in a replay at Celtic Park and then drew Rangers who promptly beat us at Ibrox. So when, within a few weeks of coming home, I was playing in the semi final of the competition, I was actually turning out for Rangers for the first time in a Cup match in a round I'd never even reached before. To go on after that to a Hampden win and a medal must be some kind of record! Whether it is or not, though, doesn't matter too much. All that matters to me is that I have that medal at home and I want to add to it in the future with Rangers.

It was always an ambition of mine to play for Rangers. But Kilmarnock, always a good club for goalkeepers, had come along first to sign me as a youngster. Down through the years they have managed to field a succession of international or Under-21 players ... Sandy McLaughlin, Bobby Ferguson, Campbell Forsyth, myself and Alan McCulloch. The goalkeeping heritage is a bit special. By the time I was twenty I was on the fringe of the international set up.

The Scotland manager at that time was Willie Ormond and I was one of the goalkeepers he took to the World Cup Finals

His first-ever Scottish Cup Final – and yet Rangers' goalkeeper looks supremely confident here as he makes this save, watched by (from left) Rangers' Tom Forsyth, Dundee United's Davie Dodds and Rangers' Gregor Stevens

28

in West Germany. I didn't play, but I was one of the twenty-two travelling players he took to Frankfurt and that was the kind of break I had only dreamed about. I was a kind of understudy to Alan Rough for the next few years but, after playing in Chile on a pre-World Cup tour of South America, I was dropped by Ally MacLeod. I was named in the squad of forty for Argentina but left at home, relegated to a non-travelling stand-by player. I thought that my international career was over then but Jock Stein arrived at the start of the following season and he named me in his first squad, and picked me to play against Norway at Hampden in a European Championship match.

That was disastrous for me. In the opening minutes, before I'd had a chance to get used to the whole occasion, I'd lost a goal. A corner from the left beat me, went across goal to the far post and was knocked in. Eventually we won the game 3–2 when Archie Gemmill scored with a late penalty, but again I was out and then when I lost my club place at Middlesbrough any dreams I had of playing for Scotland again simply died.

It isn't so easy this time, but still Stewart makes it to the ball as Davie Dodds challenges powerfully in the air

Veteran goalkeeper Peter McCloy, who played in all the Cup games until the semi-final against Morton, prepares to get down to the ball as Colin McAdam wards off the powerful threat of Aberdeen defender Doug Rougvie

It looks as if Jim Stewart is going the wrong way – but he recovered and again the new keeper stopped Dundee United scoring

Another Scotland keeper who preceded Jim Stewart in Rangers' goal, now-bearded Stewart Kennedy, still playing with Forfar. He returned to Ibrox last season in a League Cup match and is seen here saving from Derek Johnstone

Even now I'm reluctant to think about the international scene. I know that people were talking about my chances again because I had shown some good form with Rangers. But, I just want to establish myself as a first team player and get my best form back. I still have some way to go – you need time to settle in.

You need time to adjust to new surroundings and new challenges, to get used to the players who are in front of you. It's only when a real understanding develops between a goalkeeper and his defence that things go right. If, after I've had that time, Jock Stein decides to take another look at me or to pick me I'll be delighted. Obviously I'd like to add to my two international caps, but my first priority is trying to help Rangers win the trophies they want.

I feel I owe the club something. If manager John Greig had not come in to buy me, I'd still be playing away in meaningless reserve team matches in front of a few hundred fans who really couldn't care less what happens in the game. Instead I'm back in the big time – and I made it by just forty-eight hours. Rangers were just that much ahead of the transfer deadline. If they had been a couple of days later then I would have missed all that glory at the end of the season.

Now I can look forward to more big games and to playing European football as well. That's something I relish. Going into the Cup Winners' Cup is so much more than I could ever have dreamed of six months or so back. I know people talk about 'fairy tale' success stories but what else could you call what has happened to me? There is no other way to describe it as far as I'm concerned!

I had become more than a bit despondent at Middlesbrough. When you're 27 years old you know within yourself that you are reaching your peak – or should be – especially when you're a goalkeeper! It's when you're about my age that you have developed the kind of experience that goalkeepers need, and you still have a lot of time left in the game.

So I see myself as being able to give Rangers a good few years of service and, while I've been praised, I know that I can do better in these years that lie ahead. I've been congratulated for some of my performances and the fans seem to remember, in particular, a save from Eamonn Bannon of Dundee United in the first of the two Scottish Cup Final matches. It was a free kick and Bannon was given a second chance at it. The referee had ordered the kick to be retaken because our wall had broken before the ball was struck. Anyhow, he had another go, got the ball past our line up and I saw it very late. I just managed to get one hand to the ball and push it over the bar. OK, it was a good save – but I hope I'm able to make a lot more like that one. That's what I'm in the team to do after all.

A lot of fuss is made about goalkeepers' mistakes and it's true to say that our mistakes are highlighted. It's a very lonely job at times. Other players can make their mistakes in less vital areas and no one notices them. If a keeper makes a mistake then everyone sees it. And if the TV cameras are at the game then they see it again and again.

That kind of thing can haunt you. But you just have to learn to live with it. If you do happen to make a mistake no one knows it better than you do anyway. I know how badly I felt in that international game at Hampden against Norway. If we had lost I would have blamed myself and I have never been as happy as when wee Archie scored the goals which gave us both points. OK, I lost my place but Scotland didn't lose the game and that was very, very important to me.

I had a taste of Europe with Rangers last season – just enough to whet my appetite for the matches to come which mean so much to a club with Rangers' reputation abroad. The Boss, John Greig, arranged a trip to Portugal for the team and we played against Estoril. It wasn't a vitally important game in itself but the Boss was able to try out one or two tactical ideas and I was able to get to know the players better. A trip abroad like that when you are living as well as training together can be important. It helped me settle in that bit more quickly and work out some things with the defenders who were playing in front of me, and also gave me a glimpse of how Rangers do things when they travel abroad.

Basically I know that I've been lucky enough to join one of the greatest clubs in the country. I don't mean only Scotland when I say that – I mean the whole of Britain.

Players talk about the glamour of the English First Division and the set up down there which, with top clubs like Manchester United or Liverpool, is fair enough. But I was with one of the less-fashionable clubs, Middlesbrough, and even when I was in the first team every week I didn't see anything there which puts them on a par with a club like Rangers.

At Ibrox there is a different feel about the place. Whenever you step through the front doors you can sense the tradition, and when you go out onto the field and hear those fans you know that this is a special club. And now, with the new stadium you know, too, that Rangers are not a club which is content to rest on its laurels and simply live on past glories. They want the club to be great in the modern era. The ground is going to be one of the best in Britain and it's up to the players to give

Jim Stewart reports for training with manager John Greig after signing from Middlesbrough

the fans performances to match. I know how I feel. To be rescued from obscurity and made a part of a great club like this one is unbelievable. I'll be grateful forever and do everything I can to try to give Rangers the success the club demands. That is, I'm sure, what every single player at the club wants to do as well.

We know that the fans want a League title to go alongside the Scottish Cup we won last season. So that has to be our aim . . . that and some measure of success in Europe. Rangers supporters are reared on success.

Rangers players have been reared on that diet too, as well as a very rich diet of glamour matches in Europe. All the great teams from the Continent have been to Ibrox . . . Real Madrid . . . Bayern Munich . . . Ajax of Amsterdam . . . Inter Milan . . . Fiorentina . . . Rapid Vienna . . . Anderlecht . . . Standard Liege . . . the list goes on and on. Now I'll be a part of it as we add to the list of Continental battle honours and the thought of playing against the cream of the Continent thrills me.

It's a million miles away from that works park I was playing on in my last match with Middlesbrough!

THE SPACE AGE STADIUM

When the dreams of a space age Ibrox were born it's doubtful if anyone realized the vision with which the whole ideal would be approached.

It has always seemed to me that the directors responsible for building the main stand at Ibrox away back more than fifty years ago were visionaries. No less can be said about the men who have watched this current dream reach completion. In an age when football seems, at times, to be under siege, when gates are falling and the game is criticized, and hooliganism is driving decent people from the terracings, the new-look Ibrox is a declaration of faith in the future of the game – and in the future of Rangers as one of that game's most famous clubs.

The chairman Rae Simpson has gone on record as saying just that. 'It has been a massive job,' he declares. 'But it has been well worthwhile for us, and, I hope for the rest of football. This stadium can match the best in the country for facilities. We embarked on the project with that aim. Not just that, of course, but we have spent all this money because we want Rangers to remain among the greatest clubs in Europe. This is one way, we are sure, we can tell people proudly that we have faith in the future of the club.'

The cost has totalled ten million pounds, a staggering sum in these days of football's impoverishment, when the government and local authorities cannot afford to spend money on maintaining Hampden, Scotland's national stadium. And as that famous ground crumbles year after year, the new Ibrox grows at another end of the city gleaming with colour, sparkling with its three new stands and with that famous old stand still there to remind everyone of the earlier pioneers. The chandeliered hallway and the marble staircase will remain the same. The trophy room is untouched because tradition will always survive.

The skeleton of the last of the new stands is the backdrop to this heading duel between Joe McLaughlin of Morton and John MacDonald of Rangers. The Morton centre half wins it

Yet the area exclusively reserved for season-ticket-holding members has been given a face lift and other improvements have been made in the main building. But the bulk of the money has been spent on the new stands which will provide twenty-five thousand new seats.

Manager John Greig explains: 'We looked into everything very carefully and the conclusion reached was that supporters nowadays want more comfort. They want seats. They want to be able, say, to take their family and know that they can sit down in comfort and not have to stand around on the terracings. So that's what we have provided. In all, counting the seats in the main stand, we will have just over thirty-five thousand seats in the ground when the last of the new stands is completed. The one area where fans will still be able to stand is in the enclosure in front of the old stand. That will hold just over nine thousand so the capacity of the ground will drop to forty-five thousand. But it had to be done.

'For a start under the new ground safety act certain improvements had to be carried out. So rather than do things piecemeal we decided that great improvements could and should be made. But some kind of standing area had to be kept because there

This is the way Ibrox looked before the massive ten-million pound reconstruction was started. The sole stand then was the main one on the right. Now the ground will boast four stands

are supporters who prefer to stand. We realized that and we have kept the enclosure for them.

'But seating was our priority. Apart from the advantages of comfort which are offered to the fans we knew from various reports that seating could help stop trouble at the ground. And this has been the case. The police have consulted with us regularly and naturally they have been delighted at the results so far. The number of arrests in the new stands has been very, very few. In that sense alone, this has been a success.

'There have been other successes as well. The kids who came along to the newest of the two stands last year were given a little souvenir when they came in and that worked too. We saw an increase in the number of people bringing their youngsters along to the matches. That's what we want. These kids will be the supporters in years to come.'

That kind of forward thinking will develop even more. Plans are being made to provide all kinds of family tickets or children's tickets and this has been made much easier now that clubs in Scotland will be keeping their home gates. There is no limit to the ideas which could be put into operation. Advance booking of seats, possibly even on a computer basis, could become a reality too once the last of the three new stands has been completed.

Club secretary Campbell Ogilvie explains: 'The season has to open without the whole capacity being available. Work will still

have to be completed on the last and biggest of the three new stands. But there are ideas in hand. We have looked at the States, Europe and down south at England and various ideas which appeal to us will be incorporated eventually.

'We have a new ticket office at the ground already and by keeping our home gates it makes it a great deal easier to use different methods of ticket selling in advance for certain sections of the stands. We did have a family section in the newest of the two stands last season and this kind of thing can be developed. We know that the stadium is going to be the best and most modern in Britain so the marketing aspect has to be in line with that.'

Already the 'marketing' includes offices under the two new stands rented by various companies who find Ibrox a better site than central Glasgow. And sponsors are being invited to back various matches throughout the season.

Manager John Greig explains: 'The sponsors idea has been successful in England, at places like Liverpool. What happens here is that a company can bring along their guests, see around the stadium before a game, have a special lunch laid on and then take over a special function room which is sited in the main stand. Tickets for the main stand are, of course, part of the deal. It has worked out well so far and we shall be continuing to develop this kind of idea.

'As for the offices under the stands. Well, it was space which might otherwise have been wasted because we have gymnasium facilities under the main stand and we have a training ground just across the street. The club didn't need extra space, but to have it lying unused week after week would have been crazy. The Continentals have shown us that a stadium has to be used to generate revenue all the time and must not just lie empty between games. So we have these firms who rent offices from us and it is another source of valuable revenue. In the modern game this is all essential. After all the club has made a very, very big investment in this ground. Ten million pounds is a lot of cash and making full use of all the facilities is vital for us.'

Greig is well aware that he must ensure the seats are filled on match day. 'As team manager it has to be my job to get people in through the turnstiles. We have to get backsides on all these seats,' he tells you. 'Last year we did well with gates until a late League slump when they dropped. But until then we had been getting gates of around twenty-five thousand all the time. With European games we can do even better this season. I know people say the stadium could have been bigger, but under the new safety laws the crowds would have been cut considerably

Ally Dawson clears from Celtic striker Frank McGarvey. The Parkhead scoring ace says he has never experienced anything like the noise at the 'new Ibrox' during Old Firm clashes

anyhow. Our capacity would not have been the eighty thousand it was ten years ago. We opted for maximum comfort knowing that on only a handful of occasions a year would we be looking for more than forty-five thousand fans. Certain European games would come into that category, the Old Firm games with Celtic, the odd games with other leading clubs. Last year we did have several sell-outs.

'The gates were shut twice when we played Aberdeen and, of course, against Celtic we were sold out for the two games. But the stadium was holding just over 34,000 last year. We know from the past that the stimulus of European competition can encourage the crowds for other games too. A run in Europe sustains interest throughout a season and as a spin off helps domestic matches too. That's why it was important to be in Europe. Not just pride. . .but for financial reasons too.'

As well as the stands, Rangers spent the close season installing a new system of underground heating at Ibrox. It's a Swedish system which involves hot water being sent through a network of pipes laid beneath the turf. Twenty-three miles of piping were laid and vast new boilers were installed to ensure that in seasons to come there will be no games postponed at Ibrox because of frost.

Rangers chose this system after careful consideration. They travelled around various clubs in England where different forms of ground protection are in use. They saw the electric blanket, they saw the other type of blanket which is laid across the park when frost is threatened and they saw this Swedish type. They plumped for the latter because they identified flaws in the other systems which might have created problems for the ground.

It was essential to adopt some system of ground protection,

No, it's not Superman – just Ibrox veteran Sandy Jardine joking in front of the newest of the three stands. That huge girder is the biggest ever used in the construction of a football stand

because the new look stadium, almost completely closed in, would have suffered much more than others through frost. With the roofs of the four stands looming over the pitch the sun could not have got at the ground and even a mild frost might have forced postponements.

Last year there were postponements and because of the way the other fixtures worked out Rangers went for a long spell without playing vital home games. Says Greig: 'This new system means that no games will be postponed in future because of frost. And the pipes are laid under the surface in such a way that they don't interfere with the normal preparation of the ground. Spiking can still be done if there is water to be drained because they are quite a bit below the surface. The directors spent a long time investigating the different methods and this is the one which looks best. The great thing is that supporters know that the games will be OK even if the frost is very severe.

'You will notice that certain gaps have been left at the sides of each stand where the air can come in and circulate around. We were advised to do this because we did not want to stop the normal growth of the grass. All of these little things had to be taken into consideration. But we took our time over it and we believe that we have got it right.'

Go back to the new stands and there are other innovations, again with the fans in mind. Television sets have been installed to allow people to see the sports programmes while they wait for the game to kick-off. The catering facilities have been up-dated and old fashioned pie and bovril are being replaced by other snacks. Always the Ibrox emphasis is on comfort, on improvements for the fans.

And the fans have responded well so far. They like the seats. They like to be able to see the television sport while they wait for the kick-off. They like to hear the racing results announced before the game and at half time. They revel in the fact that their team, the Rangers, have the best stadium in the country.

Not only that, they know, too, that the ground has a unique atmosphere. The architects who designed the stands did so in such a way that the ground becomes a fearsome bowl of noise which increases the atmosphere at big games. Celtic star forward Frank McGarvey admitted to me after playing there last season – 'I've never heard anything like the noise there. I've played in front of bigger crowds but the sound when you are down there on the park is frightening.'

That was with thirty-four thousand people. . .add another eleven thousand to that and the Ibrox Roar can become another weapon for the team.

THE STARS OF THE FUTURE

When Rangers' manager John Greig brought his old team-mate Davie Provan back to Ibrox it was a determined move to develop the youth policy of the club.

Provan had been at St Mirren where, with another former Ranger, Alex Ferguson, now boss of Aberdeen, he worked to build the Paisley club on the basis of a sound and progressive youth programme. He guided the careers of several of the Paisley players who are now regulars in the side – Mark Fulton, Alan Logan, Phil McAveety and Dougie Bell who has moved on to play in Aberdeen's Premier League side. And Provan admits: 'They all played in the St Mirren youth team together and here it is two years or so later and they are playing at the very top of the game in Scotland. It gives you a kick, just seeing them all come through and making it. That's why it can be such a rewarding job looking after the young players. You can watch them grow, watch them mature and see them put into action some of the things you have tried to teach them.'

There are frustrations, too. Provan knows that. He sees the crucial age for young players as being between 15 and 17. In that spell a kid can stand still in terms of ability or progress enormously.

He points out: 'How many players have you seen starring for the Scotland schoolboys team, say in the Wembley match which people always seem to remember, and then you don't hear from them again. It's no one's fault. Youngsters can often peak at 15 and make no further progress after that. They can go to any club, use all the available facilities and yet still fail to make it as a top level professional. It's a mystery in a way. Other players keep progressing. Some of them who don't make it into the schools team can make it after that. There are a lot of things that have to be taken into account when you look at young players. . . . '

Ally Dawson, one of the current first-team men who came through the ranks at Ibrox

Provan won't list these in any order. But he stresses attitude and he underlines application and he takes it as read that ability and natural skills fit into the necessary attributes. Attitude, though, rates highly with the man who moulds the youngsters who may one day grace Rangers' first team. He tells you firmly: 'A boy can have all the ability in the world but if he doesn't have the right attitude then he isn't necessarily going to make it. When I talk about attitude I mean the way he behaves both on and off the field. On the field he has to be the type of player who is willing to accept responsibility and willing to help out team-mates. Off the field he has to be someone who wants to learn his trade and is willing to work hard to do just that. There is more to the game than just possessing the skills. You have to want to improve on those skills. You have to want to get back to training and work, work, work on them.

'On the skills, you naturally look to see if the player is two-footed, whether he is good in the air or not, how he reacts to the ball, whether he controls it quickly or takes time to do it. As far as pace is concerned, you see whether or not he can be speeded up with the right kind of training. All of these are important – and of course it's special to us here at Ibrox that the laddie wants to play for Rangers. That counts a great deal.'

You must also try to assess, Provan insists, how much of an idea the youngster has of the game tactically. Too often, it seems, young players are being coached badly by their schools or local youth teams. They are being regimented into formations which may not necessarily suit them and their natural skills are wasting away under the weight of too much tactical application.

Says Provan: 'There has to be a balance. People complain about coaching . . . it's not coaching they are really complaining about, it's *bad* coaching, it's wrong coaching by people who don't know the game. What we do here at Ibrox is encourage

Opposite above:
Left: Giant centre half David McPherson has a 'real chance' says Provan

Right: Billy Davies, one of the youngsters Rangers captured despite the temptations of top English clubs

Opposite below:
Left: Another player who has not appeared for the League side but could force his way through soon – striker Dougie Robertson

Right: Gordon Dalziel, only injury stopped him making a challenge for the first team last season. Now watch out for him

the players to express themselves and then gradually make them aware of what might be expected of them when they are playing in a game. You have to do that. Midfield players have to know the positions they should take up, the runs they should make. Defenders must know where to position themselves when certain situations arise during a game. Our training is geared towards teaching them that.

'They learn to support other players when they don't have the ball themselves. It's natural for youngsters to want the ball and when they are not involved with the ball, for their concentration to drop. So you devise training routines where you insist that their concentration doesn't falter. You have three against three situations, or three against two situations where defenders are in opposition to forwards. Then you use maybe one touch games or two touch games where they sharpen their skills. You make them practise shooting because it is quite amazing the number of boys who don't know how to strike the ball properly. OK, they can hit the ball well but they don't strike it as cleanly and as accurately as they should. So that is worked on, too.'

Provan arranges for the youngsters who are not on the staff full time to come in at nights and at weekends for soccer clinics to sort out their problems, where they are helped to work on their weaknesses – and also on their strengths. 'You don't ignore strengths,' says the one time Rangers and Scotland left back. 'If a lad has a great left foot you don't just make him work on the other one. That's not the way. You maybe work him harder on the weaker foot – but you build on the strengths too. You make them even better than they are naturally. That is important.'

The boys Rangers sign are getting younger. It's not unusual for 13 year olds to be attached to the club; not unusual for them to sign boys of that age and work them through the system as they sift out the stars of tomorrow.

Afternoon sessions are used to hone the skills of the youngsters who are on the ground staff. And Provan feels that these 'overtime' work-outs are essential. He believes that young players don't want to work at the game as hard as they used to.

'It doesn't come easy,' he claims. 'There is no easy way to be a top-class football star, no matter how much skill you have as a schoolboy. You must ally that to hard work. If you don't then you won't make it to the top. We stress this to the boys and it's amazing how many of them do extra work voluntarily. They want to improve – and that's back to the question of attitude mentioned earlier. There is no substitute for that.'

There were times last year when the reserve team had an

48

Opposite: Iron man defender Tom Forsyth wins this challenge with Dundee United striker Paul Sturrock, the star he tamed in the two Cup Finals

It's Willie Johnston back in Hampden action during the first Cup Final clash with Dundee United. The Tannadice player racing in is midfielder Iain Phillip

Little Tommy McLean, whose brother Jim bossed Dundee United to the Hampden Final, clashes with Eamonn Bannon

Robert Russell, harried by Dundee United's Davie Dodds, looks ready to leave this danger to Tom Forsyth

Opposite: The Rangers players celebrate at Hampden with the Scottish Cup

The confidence and courage of goalkeeper Jim Stewart is seen here as he foils Dundee United and Scotland striker Paul Sturrock

Rangers' striker John MacDonald hits the ball past Dundee United keeper Hamish McAlpine as the Ibrox men stride to Scottish Cup triumph

Veteran Sandy Jardine shows that he still has enough pace to stop Dundee United's Willie Pettigrew

Rangers' striker Colin McAdam who signed for the Ibrox club last season

Opposite: Rangers' highest priced player, Ian Redford

Opposite: Robert Russell has evaded one tackle and tries to carry the ball clear of Dundee United skipper Paul Hegarty

A midfield duel between United's Eamonn Bannon and Jim Bett in the Hampden Final

Veteran centre half Colin Jackson

Left: The man who lifted the Cup for Rangers – team captain Ally Dawson

average age of around 18 years old – and they still finished runners-up to Celtic in their League. Not only that, they scored close to a hundred goals in the competitive matches they played. Says Provan: 'That was very encouraging. These are young boys and here they are going out and playing usually against much more experienced players but they are able to hammer in all these goals.

'I know that John Greig had to change the reserve team about considerably when he took over as manager. He felt that there were too many players in the side who were not going to get through to the first team. They had been there too long. So he changed it and now we have young players and soon they will be challenging. It doesn't happen overnight. There is no magic wand. A youth policy has to be based on hard work.'

Last season there were signs of players who were ready to burst onto the first team scene. Only injuries stopped Gordon Dalziel and Douglas Robertson making their marks. Robertson was moved from outside right to centre around halfway through the season and then went off for a cartilage operation, yet still scored more than twenty goals – impressive for an 18 year old. He is one player Provan thinks will make the breakthrough. There are others. . . .

Centre half David McPherson a 17-year-old six-footer was called up during last season. Says Provan: 'He is big, two-footed and so cool. The boy has a real chance. He is a little weak in the air still but he is working hard to improve on that. We had him on an 'S' form but we had to call him up from Gartcosh because he was making so much progress. There was no way he could go much further with them so he came here and has improved enormously.'

Midfield man Billy Davies, another 17 year old, was chased by Manchester United and Nottingham Forest but opted for Ibrox. Says Provan: 'His natural skills are magnificent. All Billy needs is a little time to mature, to build his strength and then he'll be pushing for a first-team spot. His ability is unbelievable. He can do anything with the ball – and, again, he is back here working at his game even when he doesn't have to be.'

Kenny Black, a left back whose father once played juvenile football with Provan, comes from Larbert and has forced his way into the Scotland youth team. 'I wasn't surprised at the progress he made,' contends Provan. 'We let him play junior for a spell.

'He was with Linlithgow Rose, a crack junior team and we told him he could stay there until their run in the Scottish Junior Cup was over. Then he stepped up and he hasn't looked back.

Opposite: Wing wizard Davie Cooper whose artistry dominated the Scottish Cup Final replay

50

He uses the ball well and he can defend too. I can see him coming through very, very quickly.'

There are two goalkeepers, too, both of them recognized by Scotland at youth level: Gordon Marshall the 17 year old whose father once played in the same position for Hearts and Newcastle United; and 16-year-old Andy Bruce who played for the Scotland Schools at Wembley the other year and is being tipped to pick up more representative honours as he studies that most exacting of positions. Provan explains: 'The goalkeepers are given special training. There is no use coaching them in the same way as other players. It is a specialized role – highly specialized in fact – and so all the goalkeepers work-out together

An example for the Ibrox babes – John MacDonald was signed from school and here he is scoring against Morton at Cappielow. Goalkeeper Roy Baines is moving in the right direction but he wasn't able to stop the youngster's left foot drive

and then they join the others for shooting practice and for work at cutting out cross balls and organizing a defence. They have to work very, very hard indeed.'

Among the still younger crop of starlets is another goalkeeper, John Thomson, who is 15, and youngest of all 14-year-old Derek Ferguson of Burnbank who was signed when he was just 13 years old. He plays in midfield and is tipped for the top along with two members of last season's Under-15 Scottish Schools team, Gordon Sutherland from Cumbernauld and Hugh Brown from Larkhall.

Rangers don't have a regular youth team. The set up in Scotland does not encourage that as it does on the Continent. But their players do get together reasonably regularly and Provan admits to being delighted at the interest the first team men show in the boys. 'We had a game last year when our 15 and 16 year olds took on the Glasgow schools select and Robert Russell, Ally Dawson and Ian Redford were there to watch and encourage the lads. It said a lot for the spirit in the club I suppose. It also showed these boys that the established players had accepted them as part of Rangers. Having them standing there on the sidelines was the kind of boost the kids like to get. And they had done it all off their own bats.'

It was, again, down to 'attitude', that almost indefinable quality which can turn the good schoolboy player into the international star of tomorrow, which can produce the players that Rangers want to build a brave new football world well into the eighties.

Provan hopes to see the youth policy flowering inside the next year. That's when the boys who have been groomed will be knocking at the door of the first team; when all the hours of training, trips to Europe to play in youth tournaments and learn still more from the Continentals, the patient, hard work may pay off in the best way possible – by turning a boy into a Rangers first-team regular.

WHY I CAME BACK TO RANGERS
by Willie Johnston

When Willie Johnston returned to Rangers at the start of last
season it was almost as if the little wing hero had never been
away. Immediately he was installed as the fans' hero, the status
he had held when he was transferred to West Bromwich Albion
some eight years earlier. . . .

   Johnston had moved on to further his career in England after
starring with Rangers in the memorable season in which they
won the European Cup Winners' Cup. Johnston had been a
major personality in that side. . .he went on to become the same
with West Brom and then, again, on the other side of the
Atlantic with Vancouver Whitecaps. With the Canadian side he
added to his lengthy list of honours when Whitecaps won the

The wing wanderer who returned to Ibrox, Rangers' veteran outside
left Willie Johnston

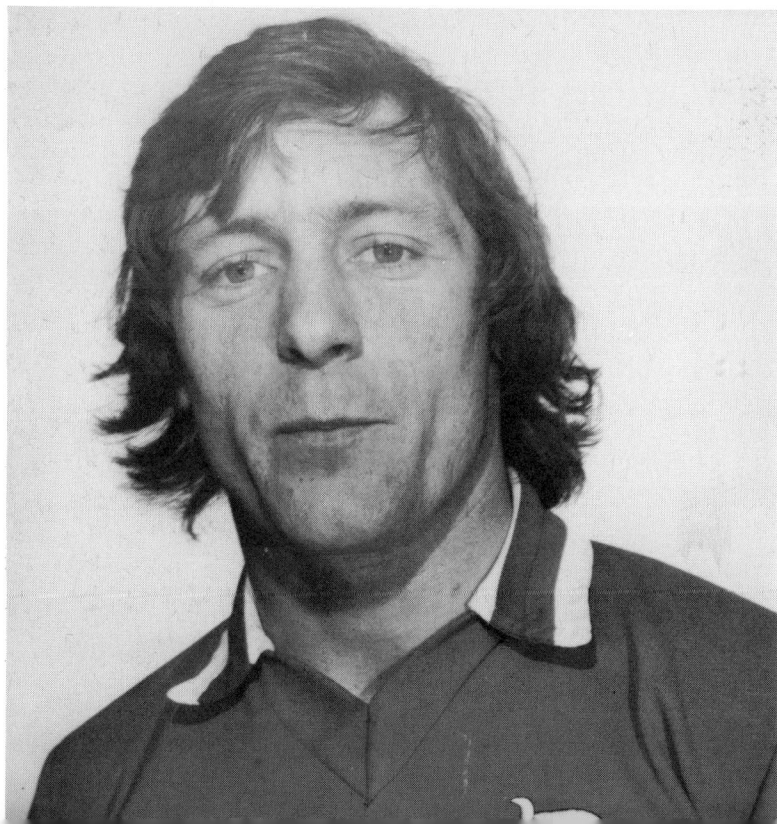

Super Bowl after beating the fabulous New York Cosmos in a marathon semi-final. Here Johnston talks to editor Ken Gallacher about his glittering and often controversial career. . . .

GALLACHER – You had a few choices open to you when you returned from the Whitecaps at the start of last season. Why did you choose to return to Rangers?

JOHNSTON – That's simple enough – Rangers are my team. They always have been my team and they always will be. I supported them when I was a youngster and I signed for them when I was only 16 years old. OK, I moved on for a spell but they stayed my team.

Honestly the lads at West Brom used to kid the life out of me about it. After every game when we got back to the dressing-rooms the very first result I wanted to know was the Rangers one. It was even like that when I was over in Vancouver. So when John Greig came in to buy me that was it as far as I was concerned. No one else had a chance.

GALLACHER – There were other clubs who wanted you, though, weren't there?

JOHNSTON – Oh, yes, quite a few down in England wanted me and with my family settled down there at that time some of the options were tempting. I had played with Alan Ball at Vancouver and got on great with him so when he asked me to go to Blackpool I seriously considered it. But like I say when Rangers came into the picture I told Bally that I had to go back to Ibrox. I'd started there and the thought of coming back to end my career with Rangers was nice. And, by the way, I don't regret it. I feel at home at Ibrox.

GALLACHER – Yet you did ask to be transferred after that European Cup Winners' Cup win and you were away for a long spell. . . .

JOHNSTON – There were special circumstances about that move. Honestly, I didn't really want to leave but I had been in trouble with referees a lot and it seemed to me that I was being victimized a little bit. I was picking up longer and longer suspensions and all I could see was more trouble looming ahead. Getting away from all that seemed the most important thing at the time, and Mr Waddell who was the manager then understood. He gave me good advice. As it turned out I think I became a better player when I moved south.

GALLACHER – Why was that?

Referee David Murdoch, who retired in mid-season, helps up Willie Johnston as Morton keeper Roy Baines watches

JOHNSTON – Well, I suppose too much came too soon for me when I joined Rangers first of all. I was in the first team when I was only 17 . . . playing for Scotland when Jock Stein was manager when I was 18 . . . and winning all sorts of medals at Ibrox. I had natural ability and I got by on that because I was a Rangers player. When I went to West Brom they were struggling a bit and so I had to become a much more disciplined player.

Looking back I don't think I was really a good player, a thinking player if you like, until I was about 28 years old. Then for three or four years after that I was probably at my best. OK, now I still have my pace over short distances but I can't run as long as I used to. The good thing is that I learned in my spell with West Brom how to conserve strength, how to use the pace in limited bursts instead of using it all up stupidly.

GALLACHER – When you say you became a better player, do you mean in a tactical sense?

JOHNSTON – Exactly. Ten years ago in Scotland we didn't

The sight that full backs fear and the man in trouble here is Aberdeen youngster Derek Hamilton as Willie Johnston carries the ball towards him

have to work too hard on that side of the game. Honestly, we didn't and as I pointed out I was winning cups and medals solely because I had natural ability. It took Don Howe, who was my first boss at West Brom, to get me thinking about the game. He was the one who used to tell me that I couldn't play. He gave me stick – but he did it to get me thinking about what was required of a winger, and it wasn't just to stand out there on the line waiting for the ball.

Those days were over. When we lost the ball then I had to get back there to help out the defence if necessary. And I had to learn to use the ball more intelligently when I did get it. It wasn't just a case of haring up the wing and hitting in a cross. I had to learn how to vary my game. These things have stayed with me and they are a big help to me at the stage of my career which I've reached now.

GALLACHER – Don Howe, who was a first-class full back himself, was clearly a big influence on you at that time. Have there been other influences on your career?

JOHNSTON – I suppose there have been three main influences when I get down to thinking about that. Don Howe for the reasons I've given. You mention that he was a full back and I think that was one of the reasons he was able to help me so much. He knew the way wingers had troubled him when he was a player and he marked my card on that. It was good. You know, I enjoyed learning the game all over again. . . .

After Don Howe left, Johnny Giles completed another part of my education. Just playing alongside him was special. He talked to me a lot on the park because, of course, he was player/ manager then. He had started out as a winger himself and then become a midfield man. So he understood the problem wingers have and could also look at them from a different viewpoint after his step back. He would point out how I could help by dropping back into midfield – just an extension of what Don Howe had told me before. In fact Don used to keep telling me that I couldn't do what George Armstrong had done for Arsenal.

Armstrong had been the winger at Highbury when Don was coach there and the team won the double. Don used to go on and on about how Armstrong would drop deep and work in there and help set things up from these positions, too. I got fed up hearing about him – but it worked because I saw what Don was getting at. Then Gilesy came in with the same lessons and that's what made me a better player I think.

The other big influence on me was Mr Waddell, who is now a director of Rangers, but who was manager when I had some troubled times. He was great to me. I used to be up seeing him just about every week. If I was playing badly I would be asking him to drop me, to give me a rest, to let me have a break and find my form in the reserves. But he would never do that. He'd encourage me. He'd tell me to get my head up and get on with it. He'd tell me that he knew I would get the form back if I worked hard and didn't let myself be influenced by anything off the field. He was almost always right and he talked me through a lot of difficult times. I don't know how he did it – but he could get the best out of me. I appreciate that even more today when I look back because I must have been a handful for him. But he never once gave up on me.

GALLACHER – How about your spell in the States? How good was that for you?

JOHNSTON – It was an experience I would never have missed. I won't let anyone knock the game over there because I played with and against and awful lot of very good players.

It wouldn't be the same Willie Johnston without controversy and here he is being lectured by referee Bob Valentine

Another opponent is beaten – this time Kilmarnock midfielder Ian Gibson – and another perfect cross is sent in on goal. The Willie Johnston trademark!

OK, some things are wrong about the game there, but then there are things wrong with the game in this country too. We were averaging gates of twenty-seven thousand at the Empire Games Stadium in Vancouver in the year we won the Super Bowl. That's some going for Canada. It's some going if you can do that in Britain now!

I wasn't too crazy about the astro turf. At times it could be a help to me with my pace but you could pick up nasty burns from it if you went down. And it affected your legs badly. You tired more quickly and I heard when I was there that the fellows who play American football were complaining about it too because it had been discovered that there was a legacy of muscle injuries left by playing on that kind of surface. You had to adapt your game to suit it, which is fine, but the injury bit is worrying.

GALLACHER – Was the Super Bowl win your best memory over there?

JOHNSTON – Of course, but the semi-final was a bigger thing than the Final because it was then that we had to play New York Cosmos and what a game that turned out to be. It was a

59

two-legged game and we won the first one in Vancouver and then had to go to New York for the second leg. It lasted nearly four hours. You probably won't believe that but it's true. You see, the Americans have to get a result in their games and this means shoot-outs. But in the semi-final it also meant extra time. And by the time the whole thing was over and we had won after extra time and after the second lot of shoot-out penalties, we were all exhausted. Nearly four hours in front of a huge crowd and all that tension – but we won and then went on to beat Tampa Bay Rowdies in the Final.

The Cosmos team had all the big names and they were the favourites, so probably that's why that match stands out even more than the Final itself. You know, they had Carlos Alberton of Brazil and Franz Beckenbauer and Giorgio Chinaglia. That's what I meant when I said earlier that you came up against a lot of very good players. And, of course, I was playing with Alan Ball at Vancouver which was good for me again. You kept coming up against top-class players you had last seen playing in a European Cup match. There they all were trying to establish the game over there and in a lot of places they were succeeding. The standard was a lot higher than people here imagine. I was impressed and the number of youngsters taking up the game was impressive too.

GALLACHER – How about other memories? You know, memories from games here at home.

JOHNSTON – Well, with West Brom I think that the season we reached the semi-final of the English FA Cup was the best we had. Actually we were a bit unlucky then. I really thought that we were going to Wembley that year. Instead we lost to Ipswich in the semi and they went on to win the Cup. It wasn't only me, by the way, who thought we would win. Everyone felt the same way. We had a good side and we were playing so well. Then Ipswich beat us by one goal and it was all over. I would have liked to play in that Final. That is one regret I have – that I missed playing in a Wembley final. Still I did play there for Scotland and we won so that was a good consolation prize!

GALLACHER – And with Rangers?

JOHNSTON – It has to be the season we won the Cup Winners' Cup – not just the Final in Barcelona, although that was memorable, but the whole season. The draws we had all the way through were so difficult and yet we got to the Final and won the Cup after so many years of trying. We played Rennes of France in the first round and they were a fair side. After that, though, every club we drew was a top name in Europe – Sporting Club from Portugal in the second round when we won on the away goals rule; Torino of Italy whose team included half a dozen Italian international players and then, in the semi-final, Bayern Munich of West Germany. Again they had so many good players including Beckenbauer and the goalkeeper Sepp Maier and Gerd Muller up front. In fact seven or eight of the Bayern team we defeated went to Wembley a few weeks later and played for West Germany when they knocked England out of the European Championship. That was how high the standard of the opposition was.

Then, of course, we met the Russians, Moscow Dynamo, in the Final and I scored two of the goals. So, that has to be the year I remember best. I think any of the lads who were in that team would say the same. It was all so very special. Remember Rangers had been playing in Europe for fifteen years and had twice reached the Final of that same tournament only to lose out, first to Fiorentina of Italy and then to Bayern in a game which went to extra time. Winning in Europe had become something that the club really wanted to do so much. . . .

Off up the wing, just as in his early years at Ibrox! Even now no one can use the old-fashioned wing skills as well as Willie Johnston

GALLACHER – The team has changed a lot since those days at Ibrox and new faces have arrived. Which of the new players have impressed you since you came back last season?

JOHNSTON – There are a few and some of the younger lads especially. John MacDonald, Ian Redford and Jim Bett are three of them. John is still a teenager while Ian is only 21 and Jim just a year older than that. So these are the players for the future I suppose.

John gets goals – and that's something I always rate as the most difficult job in the game. Yet he seems able to knock them in regularly and without a trace of nerves. As far as I'm concerned that is a priceless asset. He is going to get better and better once he puts on a little more weight. He is also the kind of boy who is willing to work hard at the game, always trying to improve on his basic skills. He could go all the way to the top.

Ian Redford puts in more work than any other player in the

Young John MacDonald may be losing the ball to Airdrie midfield man Tommy Walker here, but John remains one of Willie Johnston's tips for the top

team I think. He just runs and runs and, again, he works hard to improve his game. Maybe Ian just tries that little bit too hard and once he learns to harness the energy he has he could be a better player. That comes from experience and he is picking up valuable experience all the time. He has looked good in midfield and up front as well. He is going to become a very good player for Rangers.

Jim Bett reached Ibrox after a spell in Belgian football and that Continental approach is stamped across his play. He has the kind of patience and knowledge that the Continentals apply to their game, so it has taken time for him to settle because in our League it's still 100 miles per hour.

The teams here want to play all out all the time and the game isn't meant to be played that way. Jim has the right ideas because he learned them on the Continent. His ability and his thoughts about the game and his approach have all come from his Belgian experience.

GALLACHER – Do you prefer that Continental approach?

JOHNSTON – In many ways I do. I think that the Premier League here is far too serious. There is so much at stake for the ten teams involved and playing each other four times a season in the League isn't a good thing. You get too familiar with each other's styles. And it could be six or seven meetings if the Cup tournaments are included.

The other thing is the business of tackling from behind. Front players don't have the chance to show their skills because they know that some six foot defender weighing fourteen stones is behind them ready to whack them whenever the ball is played forward. It's not on, that. There has to be a ban on that kind of tackle if people want to see skills flourish because they won't under the present circumstances.

GALLACHER – What other changes have you seen in the years you have been away?

JOHNSTON – The teams in Scotland are more tactically aware now. Sometimes that's only in a defensive way but there is still more thought put into the game. But I did prefer the other League set up. I don't enjoy the game as much with the top ten arrangement.

Oh, and the other big change is in Ibrox itself. What a stadium it is now! Once the third stand has been finished it will be as good as any ground I've played in – and I've played in a few. Honestly, I think it has to be as good as any of the big stadiums in Europe, or even in the States. That has impressed me. I'm just happy that I have been given the opportunity to come back and to play here before my career ends.

BRIGHT BEGINNINGS– THEN A FIGHT FOR EUROPE!

For most clubs qualification for one of the prestigious, money-spinning European tournaments is a bonus. It provides their players with fresh challenges . . . their supporters with glamorous opposition . . . and the club with a financial boost.

But for Rangers, Europe is not a bonus. Playing in Europe each season is just what is expected of the team and that is why manager John Greig was determined last season that Rangers would qualify for one of the three competitions. The year before they had failed to push themselves into any of the Continental competitions and the four places available in Scotland had gone to Aberdeen, Celtic, Dundee United and St Mirren.

As Greig emphasizes elsewhere in this book, missing out on Europe was a bitter blow to himself and the players as well as a disappointment to the Ibrox fans. All of them missed out on the kind of top class games they have been so used to hosting at Ibrox down through the years of involvement in the various tournaments.

So last season European qualification was coupled with trophy-winning at the top of the Ibrox priority list.

And when Rangers began the season in style with huge gates watching their pre-season clashes with London's top two, Arsenal and Spurs, it seemed that there would be no problems for Greig and his players.

That first game against Arsenal had 25,000 fans at Ibrox to see Colin McAdam and Jim Bett make their first appearances for the Rangers side. But while Bett looked marvellously impressive, the man who stole the show was John MacDonald with two goals, one in each half. That beat a full strength Arsenal side, missing Liam Brady certainly but parading the rest of the players who would be their regular First Division side in the following season. Pat Jennings was in goal, Brian Talbot

The early season sight which brought so much joy to Rangers fans – striker Colin McAdam celebrating one of his goals!

and Graham Rix in midfield and Alan Sunderland and Frank Stapleton were the strikers. It was an impressive line-up and they too had a new boy, million-pound-signing Clive Allen. Yet all of them were overshadowed by MacDonald whose goals were superbly taken.

Three nights later the new Ibrox stand was officially opened by Spurs and a sell-out crowd of 34,000 packed themselves into the new look stadium. Again they saluted a marvellously impressive Rangers victory. And, this time, the star was Ian Redford. He scored the first goal after only five minutes and then swept past Glenn Hoddle just after half time to set up another goal for Colin McAdam. Spurs did get one back but even the elegance and skill of Ossie Ardiles and Ricky Villa could not halt Rangers as they chalked up another notable win.

As a boost for the season's real opening the games could not have been bettered. And even when Rangers could only draw at Broomfield – against newly promoted Airdrie – in their first match, spirits still soared.

Little wonder! The new players had fitted in well. Jim Bett was spraying the ball around in midfield with authority and style. . .Colin McAdam was getting goals up front and suddenly Rangers had a winning look about them. Not only that, they also had a flowing, attractive look about their play.

Yet all of that could not help them in their first hurdle as they aimed for Europe. Winning the League Cup would have guaranteed them a place in the UEFA Cup – but after two easy victories over little Forfar Athletic they were paired with Aberdeen. A win at Ibrox with Colin McAdam grabbing the only goal of the game set them up for the return. Yet at Pittodrie, despite playing well, they went out in a storm of controversy. With Aberdeen leading 2–1 and the game seemingly set for extra time, the referee awarded the Dons a penalty. Later, TV replays revealed that the incident had been a yard outside the eighteen-yard line but no matter how long or how loud the players protested the decision stood. Gordon Strachan struck the ball home – his second penalty of the game, incidentally – and Rangers were out.

One European chance had gone, just as one trophy had also

Ian Redford in action against Morton as Cappielow midfield man Jim Rooney tries to stop this shot

Not this time! Peter McCloy clutches the ball safely as Aberdeen's Under-21 'cap', Andy Watson, comes in on goal

Captain for the latter part of the season, Ally Dawson clears from Aberdeen veteran Drew Jarvie

disappeared! It was a bad blow but the fans looked to the League for consolation and the team were powering forward strongly there as they challenged reigning champions Aberdeen. A last minute goal from Alex Miller gave them a 2–1 win over Celtic at Parkhead. They drew with Aberdeen at Ibrox in front of a sell-out crowd . . . and the signs pointed to a continued challenge on that front.

Then suddenly, swiftly, without warning Rangers slumped. A disastrous result against Chesterfield in the Anglo Scottish Cup – a tournament they had tried to avoid – helped spark off a dreadful run of results. In a six game long Premier League spell they lost two games and drew four. That run from the end of November into January meant a bleak December of despair for the Ibrox fans. It included a home defeat from Morton on an ice bound Ibrox when the Cappielow forwards controlled their feet so much better than Rangers' big defenders did. It was the first home loss of the season and it was followed by a two goal defeat from Aberdeen at Pittodrie. As well as that they could only draw with Hearts and Kilmarnock, the two teams later relegated, and with Airdrie and Partick Thistle. It was a dismal time!

Hints of a revival came and went quickly. A win over Aberdeen in front of 32,000 fans at Ibrox brought renewed hope. It lasted all of a week. The following Saturday Rangers had to travel to Tannadice and they lost there 2–1, went to Celtic Park and lost 3–1 and the high hopes they had nurtured of mounting a fierce challenge for the title had slipped away. The championship was beyond their grasp and the Cup was the one trophy left.

Yet the fight for Europe in the League was not abandoned. It couldn't be. Memories stretched back to the season before when all Rangers' hopes centred on winning the Scottish Cup. When they failed at Hampden they were left with nothing. Greig did not want an action replay of that. . . .

So he took his players away to Estoril for a break, played there, tightened things up and then returned, refreshed and ready to fight on in the League to guarantee that place at least in the UEFA Cup. It came down to a battle between Rangers and the ambitious Paisley club St Mirren. The year before, the Saints had tasted European football for the first time. They

Jim Bett, a revelation at the start of the season, holds off a challenge from Aberdeen full back Stuart Kennedy

wanted a quick return and realized that third place in the table would give them that. Rangers knew it too, though, and in a seven game spell at the end of the season they lost just once. That was to Celtic when one goal defeated them in a game which seemed destined for a no-scoring draw.

For the rest they beat Dundee United, Morton and St Mirren, drew with Aberdeen at Pittodrie, with Partick Thistle at Firhill and then the week before the Cup Final blasted four goals past Hearts. That clinched things. They had secured a place in Europe by edging ahead of St Mirren into third place in the

A clash which will be seen several times this season as Rangers' new signing, bearded John McClelland, tackles Paul Sturrock of Dundee United in the international match between Scotland and Northern Ireland. Northern Ireland skipper Martin O'Neill is on the right

table. A vastly superior goal difference made sure that Greig had what he wanted. All along the Rangers boss had insisted: 'I want to see us in Europe before we go to Hampden for the Cup Final. Dundee United have qualified through winning the League Cup and if we can qualify also then it takes some of the pressure off the big day. We can go there in a much more relaxed frame of mind than we would if we knew that the Cup remained our only hope of playing in Europe.'

Qualifying had been difficult once again. The growing pressures of the Premier League have made it that way. In the end, Rangers reached the Cup Winners' Cup with that Final win over Dundee United. But it was important to them to prove they could take the League pressures at the end and come through well. It was another test Greig had set the team – too late for the title maybe, but it was still a test of character. When they knew that Europe was at stake they responded with a spell which stressed the lost opportunities of the season.

If they had been able to maintain their early season rhythm and form. . . *if* they had been able to put together a consistent run in that black month of December when points were tossed away so carelessly. . .*if* they had been able to keep clear of injuries and suspensions. . .then perhaps they could have carried their title challenge to the last day of the season instead of having to surrender it at the beginning of February.

Still, the Cup was there as consolation, and third place in the top ten brought some satisfaction . . . but there is no doubt that Greig's major ambition remains the Premier League Championship.

Colin McAdam, number 9, scored his first-ever Old Firm goal as Rangers head for their 3–0 win at Ibrox. Celtic goalkeeper Pat Bonner is stranded as Roddie MacDonald vainly tries to stop the ball. Rangers' John MacDonald watches

STRIKING FOR RANGERS
by Colin McAdam

It seems strange to me, even now after being a Rangers player for more than a year, to realize that I'm actually playing for the club I once supported. Before you get me wrong, I know that most players tell you when they get a transfer that they have always wanted to play for the club they have just joined, that, really, this is the one club they have always supported. And I know that this can't be right all the time. You know that too, I suppose, but in my case please believe me.

And, if you don't then you can come along and meet all the people who used to take me. My father and my uncles used to stand in the same position week after week and I went with them. They had a spot in the enclosure on the right hand side of the players' tunnel and I was there with them at every game when I was a kid. Actually, the strangest thing of all is that I have finished up as a striker with Rangers because my hero when I was a kid was their centre forward Jimmy Millar. . .and yet I started off my career as a defender.

Maybe that's not one hundred percent true – I started off playing almost anywhere I could get a game. It was late in my career before I was turned into an out and out striker and that was almost by accident.

I was with Partick Thistle then and I'd been a handyman player, used almost always in defence but occasionally thrown up front in an emergency. Then a transfer deal came along in which the then Thistle boss Bertie Auld sold the main striker at Firhill, Doug Somner, to St Mirren for £100,000. Having done that Bertie didn't have a recognized target man and that's why he turned to me. My experience had been a little bit limited in that direction. At Motherwell I played there for a spell alongside Willie Pettigrew and the manager at Fir Park, Willie McLean, had persevered with me for quite a while before I finally dropped back once more to defence.

Bertie Auld was the first man to decide that my role in the game was to be goal scorer, an out and out target man for Partick Thistle.

It didn't worry me over much. I played once or twice and enjoyed it and then he began to work on me and the more work I did the more I enjoyed the whole idea. At that time Jim Melrose was the other striker and Bertie had us out there working away together, timing runs, learning when to take diagonal runs and cross each other to deceive defenders. And little Donald Park was delegated to work with us firing over cross after cross until I could time my headers right and Jim and I could make up our minds which ball we preferred to go for. It was a whole new beginning for my career. . .mainly because I started getting goals. And that's the reason Rangers showed interest in buying me.

Remember that I was 28 years of age when the transfer talk started. I had been playing senior football for ten years, moving around the smaller clubs and thinking that part-time football at Thistle was what I had to settle for. I'd started out with Dumbarton in 1970 as a defender, usually centre half or sweeper or occasionally I was pushed into midfield if they needed a hard tackler in there. I enjoyed it and I did well enough for Motherwell to come along and bid £30,000 to take me to Fir Park. That was a step up because it meant full-time football and Motherwell seemed an ambitious club at that time. Perhaps all the ambitions have not been achieved but, then, they did have big ideas and they wanted to force themselves into the top bracket of Scottish league clubs. Again I was mainly defending with occasional moves up front when Willie McLean thought I could do a job, especially when Willie Pettigrew was injured and out of action for a long spell. Finally when things didn't work out there I was sold to Thistle, reverted to part-time football and went back to my work as a gym teacher. It was the move after Doug Somner's sale which changed my whole career.

It also plunged me into the situation of being the first player in Scotland to go in front of the transfer tribunal. It was only that season that the new freedom of contract, introduced earlier in England, had come into force in Scottish soccer. My contract was up and basically I was a free agent if I was not willing to

And McAdam didn't have to wait too long for his second goal against Celtic. It's the same game and the burly Rangers striker turns away in triumph after his header goes in for goal number three. His brother Tom lies in the back of the net; the other dejected Celts are Roddie MacDonald and Pat Bonner

The Old Firm brothers in opposition. Rangers' striker Colin plays this ball, closely marked by brother Tom, the Celtic central defender

Big brother Colin of Rangers consoles wee brother Tom of Celtic as the McAdams leave the field after Rangers' 3–0 win

A typical action pose from old-fashioned striker Colin McAdam

accept the terms offered by Partick Thistle. There had been lots of talk about interest from Rangers – and from other clubs too – and I knew that this could be my last chance to hit the big time.

I turned down the Thistle offer – as a part-time club the money could not match what any full-time club might offer me. So then it became a duel of words between the clubs with yours truly caught smack dab in the middle. Thistle who had bought me from Motherwell for £20,000 now put a price tag of half a million pounds on me. Rangers made an offer of three or four times what Thistle had paid and then when the clubs could not reach agreement the whole matter went to the three-man tribunal to be settled. All that time I was left wondering what would happen. I had signed for Rangers by this time, as you are entitled to do under freedom of movement in the new contract deal, but the pressure was still on me. Honestly, I felt terrible about the whole business. In the end the tribunal placed a figure of £160,000 on me which Rangers had to pay and which meant that Thistle had made eight times their original investment. I still feel unhappy at that. I thought that the tribunal overpriced me. After all I was 28 years old, my salary was not high because I was a part-time player, I had not won any international honours, and the last time I had been sold Thistle had only valued me at £20,000. It was all a little hard to take in and it was difficult to adjust to it all, more especially as I had to change from being a part-timer with a small unfashionable club to being a full-timer with Rangers!

The transition was not easy.

People have said it before and I know it will be said again – changing from a small club in Scotland to Rangers means changing your whole life. The pressures are enormous and it takes a lot out of a player adjusting to that. I was lucky to begin with because the goals arrived early. In that part of the season when I was worried over whether I could settle or not the goals were flying in and that helped more than anything. Eventually, it also led to more problems because I found myself being marked more tightly and so towards the end of the season the goals dried up a little. It's something that happens to every striker at one time or another but, like I say, when you're with Rangers you are expected to be better than other players. You are expected to be in there scoring goals week after week. . .the demands made, basically because the club has always known success and the supporters expect success, are enormous. Yet, having said that, there is no place I would rather be playing!

Apart from the worries which affect every player who moves to Ibrox, I was also pushed into the spotlight because my brother Tom was playing with Celtic. Not only that but, after starting his career as a striker, he had dropped back to play at centre half, which threw us into direct opposition in the Old Firm games we had to play during the season. . . .

Everyone asks about that. . .how it feels playing against your brother in that kind of game. Well, I don't think it bothers either of us too much really.

We don't talk about the games at all. But we have been used

to playing against each other before. We started off together. In fact, I got Tom to come down to Dumbarton to train there after I had joined them. There were a few clubs from down south chasing him and he thought about going to Leeds but I persuaded him to train at Boghead and he signed for them too. Then he moved on to Dundee United before finally signing for Celtic. All that time, until the last couple of years or so, Tom was a striker. He was always a better player than me, more skilled I always felt, but he didn't put himself about much. I used to tell him to get in there and let the defenders know he was playing because he was a very fine player but he didn't seem to listen.

Now that he has taken a step back it's different. I don't have to tell him anything! There are times I haven't been too happy that I gave him any advice in that direction at all, because from a rather 'fine player' he has turned into a very tough central defender. And that change has come just as our positions have been reversed. . .now I'm the poor attacker who has to look out for hard tough defenders and Tom is one of them. Yet my mother still tells me not to kick Tom when we are coming up against each other. She still thinks I'm the big brother out to bully him – times have changed!

Tom made it to the Old Firm before I did and he also started to win honours and play in Europe before me. But I hope to catch him up over the next few years. . .and let's make no mistake about this, both of us moved because we wanted to win these medals.

Now I have a Scottish Cup winner's medal, won by sitting on the bench as a substitute in the replay against Dundee United. But I did play in the first clash at Hampden and a medal is a medal in anyone's language. OK, anyone is disappointed at being left out of the team but the boss, John Greig, made it plain to us all that it was a team effort and he had to pick a team he thought would win. Well, he did that and I have my first honour.

Now, though, it is on to Europe and finding out what that might hold for me and for the club. Obviously I don't have any real European experience – you don't pick that up at places like Dumbarton, Motherwell or Partick Thistle. But I've always felt that players with ambition must want to play in these big tournaments which is why I'm so happy that Rangers will be in the Cup Winners' Cup. I suppose most of us at the club feel the same way about that. We had qualified for Europe before playing in the Cup Final. By finishing third in the League we were guaranteed a place in the UEFA Cup. Now that would

Didn't he do well – Colin McAdam scores again and his expression tells how he feels as he comes away from goal with team-mate Ian Redford

have been fine – but the Cup Winners' Cup is the number two tournament and is a bit more special.

The one chance I've had of tasting European football was when the club took us to Estoril during the season. Things had been going badly and the Boss decided that a break together and a game at the same time would do us good. We played a team at the top of the Portuguese Second Division and we won. It helped broaden my own experience and that of some of the other players in the side who hadn't played in Europe before either. Not only that it helped the team.

We came home and scarcely lost a game after that. It was then I realized just how good these European trips can be for team morale and understanding. Players are living together for days at a time, talking together about the game, and when you get down to seriously thinking about it you know that this can only benefit a side. Particularly when it is a side as big as Rangers who are used to having that kind of European break during a season. The Boss kept saying that this was something the team had missed because the year before they had failed to qualify for any of the competitions. Well, that trip to Portugal simply underlined for me exactly what he meant.

And so within a year of signing I am starting to fulfil the ambitions I have held since first beginning my career with Dumbarton ten years ago. A medal and a tilt at Europe have both arrived when most players are thinking of their careers tapering off. That's another reason why I want to do well for the club – not just because I used to stand in that enclosure week after week supporting them, but because they gave me this chance. I'm the first to admit that it hasn't been easy. I mentioned earlier that players begin to mark more tightly when you are with Rangers, that clubs play defensively against the top teams in the Premier League. I know because I've been with

Aberdeen defender Stuart Kennedy finds it difficult to get to the ball as the powerful Colin McAdam shields it in a Rangers' attack against the reigning champions

clubs who have been told to do just that. But the rewards are such that there is never any way that you can complain.

The real difference is, I suppose, that when you are a part-timer with a club like Thistle you can relax a little more.

Players have another job outside the game and so football is not the be-all and end-all of their existence. They can afford to take a defeat knowing all the time that they don't have to rely on the game for a living. We can't do that. Anyhow, no one would want to do it. We have to try to keep winning because the club has always known greatness. I knew that as a youngster when Jimmy Millar and Ralphie Brand and the others were taking title after title, Cup after Cup. So we have a tradition to carry on.

People sometimes ask me if I would like to be given an international chance. The answer is obvious. Of course I would! But that kind of talk isn't going to sway me away from the real object in my life – and that is helping Rangers. Last season when I was scoring goals there was talk of being given a run out in the Under-21 team as an over-age player but because of injury it didn't happen. If it comes up again in the future then I'll be delighted. . .and maybe it could happen. After all Peter Withe of Aston Villa is around the same age as I am and he made his English debut against the Brazilians last season.

Perhaps there will be a return to the old fashioned British centre forward. Withe is most certainly that kind of player, Joe Jordan is something the same though he has more skill I think than the Villa man. He played so magnificently last season for Scotland against Israel at Hampden. I don't think I've ever seen anyone lead the line better.

And on the subject of old fashioned centre forwards isn't the West German striker Horst Hrubesch one too?

Obviously it pleases me because I'm that kind of centre forward myself. I don't believe in too many frills. I see my function as being up there in the box, battling with defenders and trying to get goals; or, if not getting them myself, then making spaces for other people to get them. If I can keep doing that for Rangers then I'll be helping pay them back for giving me my chance at the top level.

Because, playing with Rangers is the top. Just ask any of the players and they'll tell you the same. . . .

JOHN GREIG—
THE MAN IN CHARGE

For three turbulent years John Greig has been the manager of Rangers, the man in charge of the team and the gleaming new stadium.

And for these three years John Greig believes he has been learning a whole new trade . . . so new, so fresh, so challenging that even his dozen years as captain of the club had not prepared him completely for the role.

As the season closed last summer, and Greig looked at the Scottish Cup he and his players had won, he admitted: 'I'm a far better manager today than I would have been if I had come into the job and known nothing but success. I believe that the year we didn't win anything – and didn't even qualify for Europe – brought that home to me.

'I didn't like it at the time. There is no use trying to kid anyone about that! It was a terrible blow to the club being out of Europe but I think I have benefitted from having to face up to problems. I think, too, that I know more about the game now than I ever did as a player. You see things from a different perspective . . . .

'If it had all been smooth running then I would not be as good a manager as I am today.'

While Greig realizes that the one year without a trophy was a costly one for the club, he can also stress its importance as far as his own job has been concerned. Since he took over from Jock Wallace in the summer of 1978, stepping straight from the playing ranks into the manager's office, Greig has maintained that he must build his own team. That is still his objective today – and it is one he is getting closer to as every season passes.

He explains: 'I was not being disrespectful to the men that I played with when I said that in the past, nor am I being

Veteran Peter McCloy rises high above Aberdeen striker Mark McGhee at Ibrox. McCloy lost his place to Jim Stewart but Greig maintains, 'Peter got us to the semi-finals of the Scottish Cup'

83

Jim Bett, the midfield man John Greig bought from Belgian football, is chaired by two more Greig signings, Ian Redford (*left*) and Colin McAdam. Other Rangers' players are (*left to right*) Colin Jackson, Alex Miller and John MacDonald. Bett had just been named Mackinlay's Personality of the Month at the start of last season

Right: Little Tommy McLean, still a key man in certain games for Rangers. Greig says, 'his vision is marvellous'

disrespectful saying it now. They have all done tremendous jobs for the club and even this season we would not have won the Scottish Cup without some of these older players. But I think that every manager wants to be judged on what he believes to be the team he has built himself.

'Gradually I have been signing new players and things are going in the direction I want. When I also start to get ·players through from the reserve team then I'll know that the club is on the right road.

'Down through the years it has been hard for Rangers to provide players from the reserves, possibly because of the club's need for success. When we don't achieve that success then the fans are unhappy – and probably after the rich diet they have known since the club began, they have a point.

'Equally it places pressure on players. So it isn't as easy to introduce young players to the first team with Rangers as it is with other Scottish clubs – except Celtic, of course, who have similar worries to us.

'Equally it can be hard on players who come to the club, but

Striker Colin McAdam, one of Greig's new men last season, leaves one Forfar defender trailing and prepares to cross as another races in

mostly experience can carry them through the tougher times. At the moment I have a mix of players . . . there is Ally Dawson, who took over my old left back position, and young John MacDonald who I brought in at the start of my first season. Both of them have come through the reserve team.

'Then there are the players I've bought . . . Ian Redford, Gregor Stevens, Colin McAdam, Jim Bett, Jim Stewart and the newest signing John McClelland, the Northern Ireland international. Plus the players still in the squad who were there alongside me when I was team captain.

'There has been a turnover in players since I took charge and that had to be. Basically we had a lot of fair players in the reserve team who weren't quite good enough, in my opinion, for the first team. Not only that, they had been there for several years and I felt that they were blocking the progress of the younger players I wanted to try out. So quite a few of these players have moved on.'

86

That meant that Greig was able to field one of his youngest-ever reserve teams last season. Apart from the inevitable de-posed players from the first team pool, the side was composed mainly of teenagers. But this is a trend Greig wants to establish firmly over the next few years.

Rangers' Cup Final opponents, Dundee United, were forced originally by the economics of the Scottish game to concentrate on trying to rear their own players. Under their manager Jim McLean they have been outstandingly successful. Yet McLean claims that it took seven years or so before he could see the fruits of all his labours blossoming in the Premier League.

Greig won't draw up any timetable for his own youth plans. He points out: 'It's impossible to do that. Sometimes you can be lucky and find someone like John MacDonald who is able to go straight into the first team. OK, I have had to nurse John a little over the three seasons because, while he has matured mentally as a footballer of quality, he still has a bit to go to mature physically.

'Other players take longer to develop than John did. Some mature physically quicker than they do as thinking footballers. Some need coaxing through the training programmes and the games, others have to be bullied a bit. Everyone is different and therefore you cannot give any timetables for development of players.

'All I know is that I would like to see more players pushing their way towards the first team. Basically that's good for the club because when we go to sign players then they know that they will be given a chance to prove themselves. And, not just that, if they are pushing their way towards the first team then they are making the experienced players play that bit harder to keep their places.'

But while Greig is aware of the constant re-organization and searching needed to keep a club at the top, he knows, too, that Rangers are a team who cannot afford to slip too often.

'Once, just that one season without a trophy, would be enough for me,' he says wryly. 'You have no idea just how much we missed European football last season. People might talk about having too many matches . . . but when you don't have the matches that matter then you know you are losing out on something.

'I didn't realize how badly I would take it until I started to go to games involving other teams who were in Europe and I sat there thinking just how much Europe means to Rangers as a club. It means a lot to the team, too. For one thing, when we were playing two games a week at the start of the season we

a

b

c

were playing our best football of the season. It suited the players to have the two matches. When that stopped, then we lost out on some of our rhythm.

'Also we had new players in the team and they don't get to know the other lads until they are all off together on a trip abroad. It helps so much . . . which is why I took the break in Portugal towards the end of the season. I'd been looking for a game just so that I could take the players away and build the team spirit off the park. Remember we started the season with two new signings, Jim Bett and Colin McAdam, and then I also signed Jim Stewart.

'It takes time during a season for players to become accustomed to each other when all they are doing is meeting at training and then at games. I wanted the chance to develop the kind of camaraderie that can only come when you have been travelling and living together in unfamiliar surroundings.

'Anyhow, I picked on Portugal and a game in Estoril against their Second Division League leaders who are based there. I changed around all the old-established rooming arrangements and mixed the lads up just to get them talking to each other. I wanted it to be a trip to build up that off-field spirit as well as a chance to try out a little change on the field as well. It worked both ways . . . .

'We came back to go on and win the Scottish Cup and if we had lost to Dundee United at Hampden we would have qualified for Europe by finishing third in the League. We lost two games on the run-in, to Celtic and St Mirren, each by a single goal and we were a little bit unlucky on both occasions. We were able to tighten up the defence, get a better understanding going and by the time the Final replay arrived we had regained that early season rhythm and form I mentioned before.'

Greig knew by then that a Cup win was essential for the club. He admits: 'It would have been unthinkable for me to have gone two seasons without a major trophy. That Cup was so very, very important to all of us at Ibrox.

'The fans had shown us that this was the trophy they wanted

Colin Jackson was still a reliable defender for Rangers though in this sequence he loses out to the close skill of Aberdeen striker Mark McGhee:

(a) Jackson commits himself to the tackle as McGhee brings the ball under control

(b) McGhee is moving clear now and turns as Jackson goes down

(c) The Rangers veteran is beaten and McGhee takes the ball clear

Greig left John MacDonald out of the team for certain games including the Cup semi-final against Morton. But here he is in an earlier League game at Cappielow holding off a challenge from Morton's full back Davie Hayes

us to win and we knew that we had to give them something for all the loyalty they had shown us during the season. OK, the gates might have fallen towards the end when we dropped out of the League race. . .but they stayed up for the Cup matches!

'It was the trophy we had left and while most people made us outsiders I felt that we always had a good chance of beating Dundee United – though they are a team I admire a great deal.

'Anyhow, when it came around the team had the character to do the job and to do it in style. That was important, as well. We won it with a flourish. No one could suggest at the end of the day that we had not deserved to win the trophy. Basically, that has to be our aim all the time . . . to win, but to win with flair. We have to give the supporters what they want. And, besides seeing us win matches, they want to see skilful play, intelligent play and goals. They didn't get enough of these things last year. I know that – and I want it changed.'

Greig maintains that the rhythm left the team when they missed out on the two games a week schedule. He could also point to injuries which plagued the side but he doesn't do that. Instead he points to a disciplinary record which was bad and which he intends to change for the better.

Insists Greig: 'We have a strong disciplinary code inside the club and players are fined when they get themselves in bother on the field. But players were still in trouble last year and I wasn't happy about it. There were times during the year when I needed certain men and they weren't available because they had been suspended. Well, that wasn't good enough and the players have had that spelled out to them. We cannot afford to have players sitting out suspensions in the stand when we need them out there on the field.

'No way will you hear me talking about the injuries which affected us. You can't control that. But you can control the discipline of players.'

Then Greig went on to talk about some of the individual contributions made by players during the season:

Jim Stewart – 'He came in when the team was starting to go through a bad spell and he lost four goals in his first match. But he played superbly and he helped take control of the defence. He just looked so very, very safe all the time.

'I'm not taking anything away from Peter McCloy when I praise Jim. Without Peter we would not have been in the semi-finals of the Cup. He was the keeper until then.'

Jim Bett – 'His early form was a revelation – and towards the end of the season he was back touching those heights. He came from Belgian football and needed time to settle down and get used to the kind of football played in our Premier League. A very intelligent and constructive player who gave us even more scope in our midfield.'

John MacDonald – 'I was just delighted for John that he scored two goals for us in the Cup Final replay. I've tried to guide him since I took over as manager. There have been times I've had to leave him out because the physical aspect of certain games might not have suited him. And on those occasions I've felt so sorry for him because he is such a good player. The Final underlined that – if anyone needed to have the point proved. I didn't and it makes it all the more special when a youngster who you gave his first chance plays the way John did. I couldn't have been happier for any player.'

Tommy McLean – 'I was able to use Tommy in the games when I thought his special talents and his experience were going to be vital for us. I didn't try to play him in every match last season because I thought the demands on him would have been too great. But whenever I needed him he was there and he had some marvellous matches for us. He still reads the game better than anyone. His vision is absolutely marvellous.'

Colin McAdam – 'Well, Colin came from Partick Thistle where he had had a great season and scored twenty-odd goals. He did the same for us . . . but we expect that from strikers at Ibrox. If he had been able to keep up his early scoring form then he would have broken a record or two.

'I suppose that's what we will be looking for from Colin. Twenty-odd goals with Partick Thistle is tremendous . . . twenty-odd goals with Rangers is only what we are looking for.'

Then Greig added: 'There were so many players who did contribute to the eventual success. Willie Johnston whose old-fashioned wing play cannot be bettered anywhere . . . Ian Redford who worked so hard for us in different roles during the year . . . Tom Forsyth who proved himself one of the most honest players I've ever known. All Big Tam wants to do is play for Rangers and it was great to see him collect another medal. Then Colin Jackson was as ageless as ever and Davie Cooper was the star of that Cup Final replay. I have to thank all of them. Remember after all, it's the players who go out to win games. I don't win them. It's what they do out on the field that brings Cups and championships into the Ibrox trophy room.'

Greig made it plain, too, that he would not sit back and rest once he had won the Cup. A week after that win he swooped into the transfer market to surprise the fans with a shock signing – Northern Ireland defender John McClelland bought from Mansfield for £90,000.

The night the signing was completed McClelland was playing for the Irish against the Scots at Hampden in their sole British Championship match.

The fans who watched the game didn't realize that the twenty-five year old bearded six-footer had joined the Ibrox club. They learned the next morning and afterwards Greig explained: 'I have been looking to strengthen the player pool and I've wanted to do it with quality players. The worrying thing has been that either the players I am looking for just aren't available or else clubs in Scotland are simply pricing them out of the market.

'What I did here was simple. I had the player watched in England. I went down there to see him myself and then I stepped in to sign him. There were other clubs in England supposed to be interested but I was in first and the player was delighted to join up with us.

'He is basically a central defender but for Northern Ireland he has played in both full back positions and also as a defensive midfield man. In that role he has been the anchor man allowing Sammy McIlroy and Martin O'Neill to go on and do the more creative stuff. I have bought an international player at a good fee and I have a player who can play in several different positions. I've also got someone who has experience of playing abroad and that is important to us as well.'

It was just as important to McClelland who said: 'I'm delighted to be joining Rangers and full marks to the manager – he was first in with an offer which the club accepted. I'd heard talk about First Division sides down south wanting me but Rangers were too quick for them.

'Obviously what I'd been doing in the Ireland team didn't go unnoticed. I started off my career at Portadown, then moved on to Cardiff City but they released me when I was still a teenager and I went into Welsh non-league football with Bangor. After

An action shot of Jim Bett as he strides clear of a challenge from Morton's Scottish Under-21 international sweeper Neil Orr

Greig's biggest buy, Ian Redford, moving away from Aberdeen defender Derek Hamilton in a Premier League clash at Ibrox

that Billy Bingham who is the Northern Ireland manager signed me for Mansfield. Then when he took over again as international boss he picked me for the Irish team. I've won seven 'caps' and played in World Cup games as well as on tour in Australia so I have picked up a fair bit of experience which I'm sure will help me with Rangers.

'I was surprised when they came in because when you play in England it doesn't occur to you that a Scottish side might try to sign you. You start off thinking about clubs round your own area. One or two around Mansfield way were rumoured to be interested – but when Rangers came in I wasn't hanging around. This is a club I want to play for and a club I want to win medals with.'

And that underlined another part of the Greig credo when he talks about players he wants for Ibrox – 'I want players who want to play for Rangers and who have ambition – because that's what this club has. It has more ambition than any other club in the country!'

Greig has ambitions, too. He has won two of the top three trophies in Scotland, but the Premier League Championship has eluded him so far. In his first season he captured the League

94

Cup and the Scottish Cup. Last season he took the Scottish Cup back to Ibrox again. At any other club a manager could live quietly for the rest of his career on that kind of booty. At Ibrox Greig sees it only as a beginning.

'There is no way you can rest on your laurels at Ibrox,' he maintains. 'I came very close to winning the title in my first season. But I lost out in the last two years, even though we

Bearded giant John McClelland tries on a Rangers jersey for the first time as manager John Greig welcomes Northern Ireland's World Cup man to Ibrox

finished in third position in the season just past. I want better. I want to be the team on top. I know that there are powerful challenges around – from Celtic, from Aberdeen, from Dundee United, from St Mirren. We have to be bigger than any of them. Our away form was poor last season and we have to pick ourselves up away from Ibrox. At home we lost just three times, to Morton, Dundee United and Celtic.

'The only other small excuse I can offer is that we spent a long, long time away from Ibrox for League games. Some were postponed, others were just the way the fixture card panned out. But it meant when everything was taken into account that we played just two home League games between 29 November and the end of February.

'The under soil heating will help us avoid that happening again. It was a long, long gap and it came at a bad time for us, just when we were starting to lose the form we had shown at the beginning of the season.'

Greig is aware of the great traditions of Rangers. He knows that he sits behind the desk from which some of the club's greatest names have ruled. He sits there in the shadow of the legendary Bill Struth, and he accepts all of that with the same resolution he showed when he held the captaincy on the field. He knew years of disappointment as for nine seemingly endless seasons Celtic, under Jock Stein, dominated the Scottish First Division title. There is no way that he wants to see his club go back to those years of famine . . . which is why the League is important to him.

But it's doubtful if Greig's ambitions end there. For Rangers, the club he has been with for twenty-one years, Greig has an insatiable appetite for success. When one championship is won, you start planning for the next. When one Cup has been won, you look for another. When one country has been conquered, then you look to Europe.

Greig captained Rangers to their solitary success in European competition when they won the Cup Winners' Cup in Barcelona. I'm certain he would love to lead Rangers to another trophy win on the Continent . . . and another piece of immortality for himself and for Rangers Football Club.